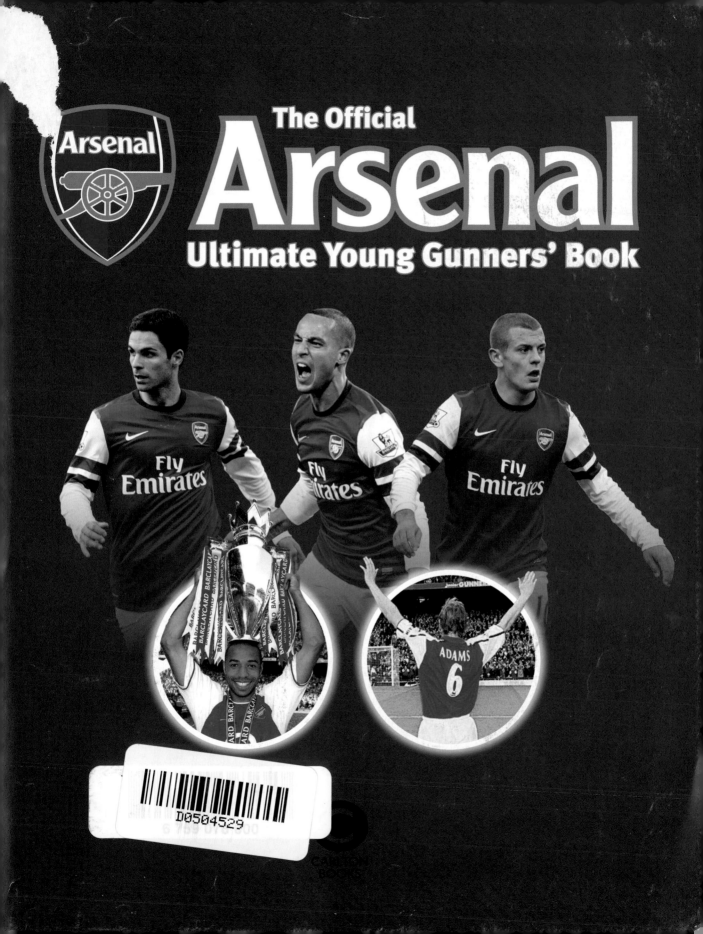

The Official
Arsenal
Ultimate Young Gunners' Book

Welcome to the ultimate guide to Arsenal Football Club!

Welcome to this official guide to your favourite football Club, Arsenal FC. It's the ultimate book for Junior Gunners, with loads of facts, stats and player profiles to enjoy.

Impress your friends and family with your knowledge of the Club – the legends, the stadiums and the trophies, then put yourself to the test with the tricky teasers and Gunners puzzles throughout the book. Plus learn and practise new skills with a little help from the Arsenal Soccer Schools coaches!

Enjoy the book and thank you for your support!

WHAT'S INSIDE?

Arsenal

My Young Gunner Profile

My name: _____

My age: _____

My favourite players (current squad):

_____

My favourite players (of all time):

_____

My playing position: My squad number:

_____

I started supporting Arsenal when I was _____ years old.

My autograph:

Place your photo here!

Club motto: "Victory Through Harmony"

Arsenal

![Arsenal crest]

FOOTBALL Club
...in numbers

2 League Cups

13 First Division And Premier League Titles

Unbeaten 2003–04

10 FA Cups

Founded 1886

1 European Fairs Cup

1 European Cup Winners' Cup

12 FA Community Shields

"If you do not believe you can do it then you have no chance at all."
Arsène Wenger

7

Our Home...
Emirates
Stadium

Home to the Gunners since the 2006–07 season kicked off, Emirates Stadium.

The first ball was kicked here in August 2005, but the stadium officially opened in October 2006.

With a whopping 60,361 seats, there's room for a whole lot more fans than at Arsenal's former stadium, Highbury.

Home team dressing room

From pitch level to the top of the roof, Emirates Stadium is over 40 metres tall – imagine ten double-decker London buses piled on top of each other!

There's so much to see in and around the ground – learn all about the Club's history at the Arsenal Museum, packed with rare memorabilia, trophies and medals, check out the statues of playing legends, Thierry Henry and Tony Adams, plus super manager Herbert Chapman or go behind the scenes with a stadium tour!

Now you're ready for kick-off. Phew!

Did you know?
The first Gunner to score at Emirates was Thierry Henry.
Who else?

Did you know?
Emirates Stadium is less than 500m down the road from old ground, Highbury!

From the skies
Check out this aerial shot of Emirates on a match day!

Pitch perfect
The Emirates' pitch is the joint-largest in the Premier League!

It really is a home away from home!

EMIRATES STADIUM

WRIGHT

ARMSTRONG

Arsenal

Fly Emirates

Gunnersaurus:
My Dino Diary

Hi, Junior Gunner!

Pleased to meet you! My name's Gunnersaurus Rex, but you can call me Gunner. I'm the official mascot to Arsenal FC. Being the mascot at the greatest Club in the world is a dream come true for me — I am definitely one lucky dinosaur.

It's my job to get the crowd going before matches at Emirates Stadium kick off, and I entertain all the fans at half-time, too. I get to travel to different countries all over the world when Arsenal or Arsenal Ladies are playing — I'm their good-luck charm.

Take a look at some of the things I've been up to recently in my photo album, or to read more about my adventures online, you can follow my blog at www.arsenal.com/juniorgunners

Big hugs,

Gunner

MORE ABOUT ME!

FULL NAME:	Gunnersaurus Rex
JOB:	Official mascot to Arsenal FC
DUTIES:	Warming up the crowd before the match and at half-time, chatting to fans, bringing good luck to the players, visiting fans in the community, representing the Gunners all over the world!
DATE OF BIRTH:	August 1993
BIRTHPLACE:	North Bank, Highbury

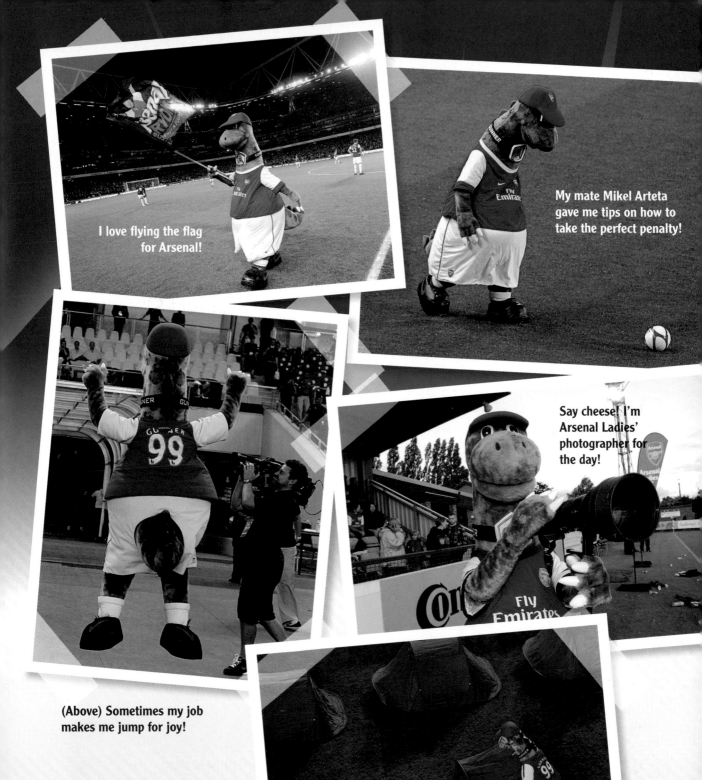

I love flying the flag for Arsenal!

My mate Mikel Arteta gave me tips on how to take the perfect penalty!

Say cheese! I'm Arsenal Ladies' photographer for the day!

(Above) Sometimes my job makes me jump for joy!

(Right) This is a photo from the Junior Gunners' sleepover on Emirates' pitch!

Spot the Ball

Look closely at this scene from a Premier League tie against Spurs. Where do you think the ball should be?

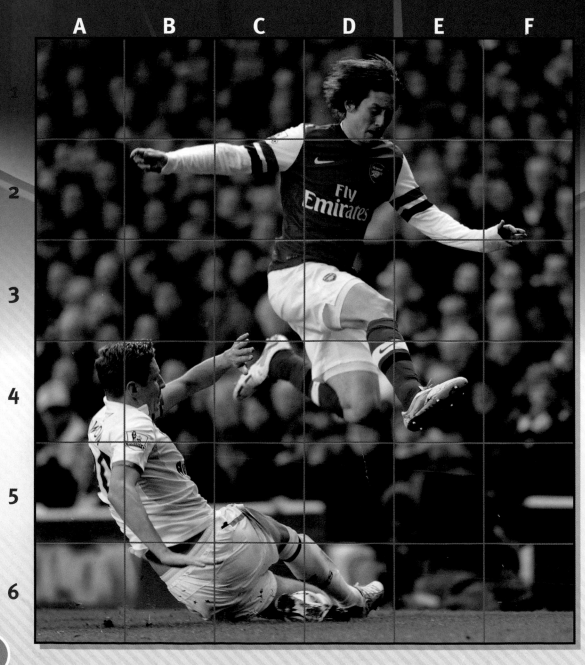

Soccer Scramble

On a piece of paper, unscramble the names of these Arsenal greats.
Tip: look through the Legends profile pages to help you.

1 INA TRIGHW

2 VIDAD EAASNM

Check your answers
to all the puzzles on
pages 94 and 95!

3 MAIL YDARB

4 RERITHY YEHNR

5 REBROT SPIRE

6 NOTY MADSA

13

Corner Close-ups

This corner routine is from a recent Premier League victory over Sunderland. All the small details can be found in the big picture. Tick the box when you find each one.

Help Gunner!

Gunner needs some help working out which two players have been mixed up here. Can you tell who they are?

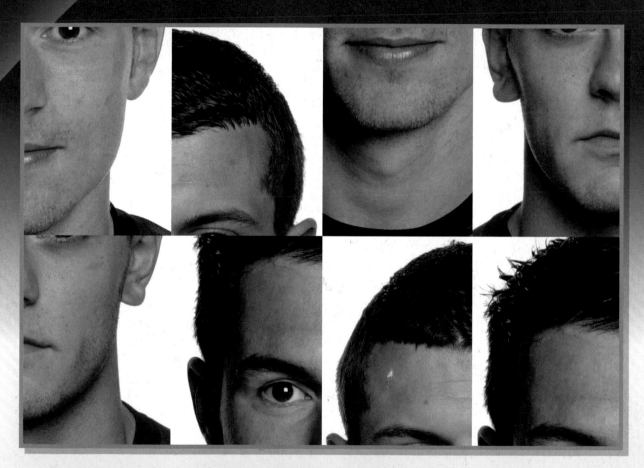

Write the names of the players here:

1 _____

2 _____

Record Breakers

Here are just some of the record breakers in the Club's history. From special players to super seasons, these stats are officially amazing! Wow your friends and family with your knowledge of the Club.

David O'Leary holds the record for the most appearances made for Arsenal – 722 MATCHES PLAYED!

The youngest-ever goalscorer was Cesc Fabregas, who netted at just 16 YEARS, 212 DAYS in the League Cup.

Thierry Henry is the Club's top goalscorer with an awesome 228 GOALS.

The most goals scored in a season was Ted Drake with 44 GOALS – a record that has stood since 1934–35!

The Gunners were the very first team in the world to have shirt numbers on players' shirts – first introduced in 1927.

ARSENAL 12

ASHFORD UNITED 0

Did you know that Jack Wilshere played in the Champions League at just 16 years old?

Arsenal's record home win was an amazing 12–0 against Ashford Utd at Woolwich over 100 years ago in 1893!

The Gunners hold the record for winning the most league and cup doubles jointly with Manchester United. Arsenal's hat-trick of doubles were won in *1970–71, 1997–98 AND 2001–02.*

Guess who is the Club's longest-serving manager? That's right, it's our very own **Arsène Wenger!**

I'm officially amazed!

Theo Walcott scored Arsenal's fastest-ever goal, clocking in at just 20 seconds in the Premier League against Queens Park Rangers in 2013!

17

THE INVINCIBLES

The 2003–04 season was a very special campaign at Arsenal FC. The manager and squad will never be forgotten for what they achieved – managing to complete a whole season unbeaten.

Wenger had built a perfect team, with Sol Campbell and Kolo Touré forming a solid central defensive partnership, Patrick Vieira as the anchor midfield man, Robert Pirès and Freddie Ljungberg building the attacks and the untouchable Dennis Bergkamp and Thierry Henry up front. Their stylish play won them the Premier League 11 points ahead of their nearest rival!

In fact, the Gunners went on to play 49 games without losing until their winning streak finally came to an end with a controversial defeat to Manchester United.

LEHMANN
1

LAUREN 12   CAMPBELL 23   TOURE 28   COLE 3

LJUNGBERG 8   VIEIRA 4   GILBERTO 19   PIRES 7

BERGKAMP 10   HENRY 14

INVINCIBLES 1ST XI

Partying… Invincibles style!

Did you know?
The Premier League commissioned a gold version of the Premier League trophy for Arsenal to keep forever!

2003–2004 SEASON *26 Wins 12 Draws 0 Losses*

Star scorer Thierry Henry celebrates just one of his many goals for 'The Invincibles'.

Did you know?
French forward Thierry Henry scored 30 of the Gunners' goals during the unbeaten run and 39 goals in all competitions that season.

Thomas VERMAELEN 5

Versatile Vermaelen is almost as good up front as he is in his natural defensive role! Although he usually plays as a cental defender, Vermaelen has covered the left-back position and likes to chip in with goals when Arsenal are on the attack, too!

The Belgian defender impressed in his first season after joining from Dutch club Ajax in summer 2009, and has since been building an ever-growing fan club. His strong performances earned him the Arsenal captaincy when Robin van Persie left the Club in August 2012, and Thomas has also skippered his country, Belgium.

PLAYER PROFILE

POSITION:	Defender
SQUAD NUMBER:	5
DATE OF BIRTH:	14 November, 1985
PREVIOUS CLUBS:	AFC Ajax Amsterdam, RKC Waalwijk (Loan), KFC Germinal Beerschot
ARSENAL DEBUT:	15 August, 2009
INTERNATIONAL TEAM:	Belgium

TRUE OR FALSE?

THOMAS IS DUTCH.

TRUE ☐ FALSE ☐ *Answer on page 94*

Ian **WRIGHT**

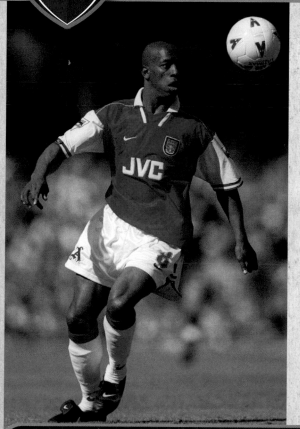

A sharp-shooting Gunner, Ian Wright notched up an amazing 185 Arsenal goals – the second highest scorer in the Club's history, behind Thierry Henry. Crowd favourite 'Ian Wright–Wright–Wright' could score goals of all types, from toe-pokes to screamers cementing his legend status among Gunners' fans.

Signed by manager George Graham, Wright made the move from south to north London in a big-money transfer. He quickly proved his worth and won the Golden Boot in his first season, scoring 29 goals. Under Graham, Wright won the FA Cup twice and League and UEFA Cup Winners' Cups once, but had to wait until he was 34 before he finally lifted the Premier League trophy as part of Arsène Wenger's squad.

Position:	Forward
Squad number:	9
Clubs played for:	Crystal Palace, West Ham Utd, Nottingham Forest (loan), Celtic, Burnley
Arsenal career:	1991–1998
Caps:	288
Goals:	185
International team:	England
International caps:	33

LEGENDS

9

PLAYER PROFILE

MY RATING

COLOUR IN THE STARS TO RATE THIS LEGEND

★ ★ ★ ★ ★

21

Lukas
PODOLSKI 9

Experienced striker Lukas Podolski joined the Club in summer 2012 from German side, FC Cologne. A natural finisher, Lukas has always been confident in front of goal, scoring over 100 goals for Arsenal and his previous Clubs. He's fast, skilful and has a clinical left foot.

His international team is Germany, although he was born in Poland. He has already represented Germany over 100 times – in three European Championships and two World Cups and he's not yet 30 years old! Lukas is looking forward to bagging lots more goals for the Gunners, too.

PLAYER PROFILE

POSITION:	Forward
SQUAD NUMBER:	9
DATE OF BIRTH:	4 June 1985
PREVIOUS CLUBS:	Bayern Munich, FC Cologne
ARSENAL DEBUT:	18 August 2012
INTERNATIONAL TEAM:	Germany

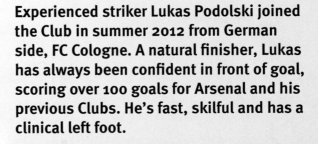

PRO PODOLSKI

IN WHICH YEAR DID LUKAS JOIN THE GUNNERS?
2010 *2012* *2013*   Answer on page 94

Thierry HENRY

INVINCIBLE

Voted top of the pile in a poll of the Gunners' greatest players, Thierry Henry is perhaps one of Arsenal's most important ever players.

One of Wenger's first signings, Thierry joined Arsenal from Juventus in 1999 to replace striker Nicolas Anelka, and had played in Italy as a left-winger. Wenger transformed Thierry into a truly outstanding striker, who went on to score a record 228 goals for the Gunners.

A star player for the Invincibles, Henry won silverware seven times with Arsenal. He went on to win the European Champions League trophy with Barcelona and was a World Cup and Euro 2000 winner with France. Quite simply a superb player.

LEGENDS

14

PLAYER PROFILE

Position:	Forward
Squad number:	14
Clubs played for:	AC Monaco, Juventus, Barcelona, New York Red Bulls
Arsenal career:	1999–2007, 2012
Caps:	377
Goals:	228
International team:	France
International caps:	123

MY RATING

COLOUR IN THE STARS TO RATE THIS LEGEND ★ ★ ★ ★ ★

23

Jack WILSHERE 10

Home-grown hero Jack joined the Arsenal Academy at the young age of nine and rose through the ranks at an astonishing pace.

Jack won a number of individual awards in his first senior season, 2008–09, earning 49 Arsenal caps. He was given the number 19 shirt, but now wears the famous number 10.

An impressive midfielder, Jack has matured into one of the most exciting players of his generation and hopes to win many more caps for both Club and his country. Wenger has already recognised Jack's leadership qualities. Who knows, one day he may even become Club Captain...!

PLAYER PROFILE

POSITION:	Midfielder
SQUAD NUMBER:	10
DATE OF BIRTH:	1 January 1992
PREVIOUS CLUBS:	Bolton Wanderers (loan)
ARSENAL DEBUT:	13 September 2008
INTERNATIONAL TEAM:	England

YOUNG GUNNER

HOW OLD WAS JACK WHEN HE JOINED THE Club?
8 ☐ 16 ☐ 18 ☐ *Answer on page 94*

Tony ADAMS

Arsenal

Tony signed for the Gunners as a schoolboy and made his debut at 17. Unlike most modern players, Adams spent his whole footballing career at Arsenal and captained the team for 14 years. He won 10 major trophies and earned over 650 caps along the way. A natural leader, his tackling was fearsome and his aerial ability was awesome – it's clear why he was such a hero at Highbury.

The day he rocketed a shot into the top corner on the final day of the 1997–98 season to crown a double-winning campaign was a great moment in Gunners' history.

Visit the Emirates and you can have your photo taken alongside the impressive bronze statue of Adams!

Position:	**Defender**
Squad number:	**5**
Clubs played for:	**Only Arsenal!**
Arsenal career:	**1983–2002**
Caps:	**669**
Goals:	**48**
International team:	**England**
International caps:	**66**

LEGENDS

5

PLAYER PROFILE

MY RATING

COLOUR IN THE STARS
TO RATE THIS LEGEND

★ ★ ★ ★ ★

Theo WALCOTT

14

Lightning-quick forward Theo joined the Club as a teenage sensation from Southampton, signing for the Gunners on his 17th birthday! He can operate as a wide-man but prefers to play as a striker, where he can beat defenders with his devastating pace.

Theo was also England's youngest-ever player, making his debut for the Three Lions aged 17 years and 75 days. He memorably scored a hat-trick for England in a World Cup Qualifier against Croatia.

Walcott wears the number 14 shirt, previously worn by fellow forward, Thierry Henry.

PLAYER PROFILE

POSITION:	Midfielder/Forward
SQUAD NUMBER:	14
DATE OF BIRTH:	16 March 1989
PREVIOUS CLUBS:	Southampton
ARSENAL DEBUT:	19 August 2006
INTERNATIONAL TEAM:	England

SPRINT KING

THEO'S BEST ASSET IS HIS...

SPEED   STRENGTH   HEADING ABILITY

Answer on page 94

Cliff BASTIN

Cliff Bastin was such a top player that he is still remembered as an Arsenal ace 80 years later. A wizard winger, he signed for manager Herbert Chapman's side when he was just 17. His goal tally of 178 is amazing if you consider that he played most of his games for Arsenal in the what was called the 'outside-left' position –left midfield – rather than as a traditional centre forward.

His glittering career was cut short by the outbreak of World War II in 1939. Had events been different Bastin may still hold the record for being the Club's top scorer.

Position:	**Outside-left**
Squad number:	**11**
Clubs played for:	**Exeter City**
Arsenal career:	**1929–1946**
Caps:	**396**
Goals:	**178**
International team:	**England**
International caps:	**21**

LEGENDS

11

PLAYER PROFILE

MY RATING

COLOUR IN THE STARS TO RATE THIS LEGEND ★ ★ ★ ★ ★

27

Olivier GIROUD

12

French striker Olivier joined the Club in the summer of 2012 along with strike partner, Lukas Podolski. A strong, physical player, Olivier is a force to be reckoned with up front. At 6 foot 4 inches tall, he is a powerful header of the ball. He not only adds height to the Gunners' attack, but has quick feet too.

In his first season with Arsenal, Giroud put in some impressive performances as well as adding important goals in the Premier League, FA Cup, League Cup and Champions League!

Olivier is a French International and has entered double figures for his number of caps with Les Bleus.

PLAYER PROFILE

POSITION:	Forward
SQUAD NUMBER:	12
DATE OF BIRTH:	30 September 1986
PREVIOUS CLUBS:	Montpellier, Tours, Istres (loan), Grenoble
ARSENAL DEBUT:	18 August 2012
INTERNATIONAL TEAM:	France

TEAM-MATE TEASER

WHICH OF THESE GUNNERS IS ALSO GIROUD'S INTERNATIONAL TEAM-MATE?
LAURENT KOSCIELNY ☐ ALEX OXLADE-CHAMBERLAIN ☐ LUKAS PODOLSKI ☐

Answer on page 94

Liam BRADY

A young Liam Brady joined Arsenal as a schoolboy and made his senior debut at 17. His combined vision, technique, strength and a lethal left-foot shot made him one of the Club's most gifted teenagers.

As the team struggled in the mid-seventies, Liam began to find his best form. His clever through-balls to the strikers helped Arsenal reach three FA Cup Finals in a row! Of these, the Gunners won the Cup in 1979, beating Manchester United 3–2.

The following year, the news that Liam was quitting Highbury for Juventus sent shockwaves around the ground. He moved to Italy for £500,000 – a huge transfer fee at the time. He went on to win the Italian League twice, but will forever be remembered as a top Gunner!

Position:	Midfielder
Squad number:	7
Clubs played for:	Juventus, Sampdoria, Inter Milan, Ascoli, West Ham Utd
Arsenal career:	1973–1980
Caps:	307
Goals:	59
International team:	Republic of Ireland
International caps:	72

LEGENDS

7

PLAYER PROFILE

MY RATING

COLOUR IN THE STARS TO RATE THIS LEGEND

★ ★ ★ ★ ★

Wojciech SZCZESNY

1

Goalkeeping runs in young keeper Wojciech Szczesny's family – his father was an international goalie for Poland and his uncle plays in between the sticks, too!

Szczesny joined the youth set-up at Arsenal as a teenager, and Wenger spotted his potential to be the number 1 keeper at Emirates Stadium early on.

Tall and strong, Szczesny is a commanding figure who organises his team-mates from the back. He made his Premier League debut in September 2010 against West Brom, and has also won 13 international caps for Poland.

PLAYER PROFILE

POSITION:	Goalkeeper
SQUAD NUMBER:	1
DATE OF BIRTH:	18 April 1990
PREVIOUS CLUBS:	Legia Warsaw, Brentford (loan)
ARSENAL DEBUT:	22 September 2009
INTERNATIONAL TEAM:	Poland

ODD ONE OUT

WHICH MEMBER OF THE SZCZESNY FAMILY IS NOT KNOWN TO BE A GOALKEEPER?
WOJCIECH'S DAD ■   HIS UNCLE ■   HIS BROTHER ■   *Answer on page 94*

Dennis BERGKAMP

INVINCIBLE

Quite simply a genius on the football pitch, Bergkamp took Arsenal to the next level, inspiring his team to win trophy after trophy in over a decade with the Club.

Gifted with the finest technical skills, Dennis the Menace was without doubt a Premier League great. He scored 120 Arsenal goals during his Highbury years – and many of them were spectacular! Dennis's creativity, poise and pure class will live long in the memory of Gunners fans.

Bergkamp's testimonial was the first match to be played at the new Emirates Stadium as a sell-out crowd turned out to watch Arsenal play his former Club, Dutch team Ajax.

Position:	Forward
Squad number:	10
Clubs played for:	Ajax, Inter Milan
Arsenal career:	1995–2006
Caps:	423
Goals:	120
International team:	Netherlands
International caps:	79

LEGENDS

10

PLAYER PROFILE

MY RATING

COLOUR IN THE STARS TO RATE THIS LEGEND

★ ★ ★ ★ ★

31

Mikel
ARTETA

8

Arsenal's Vice-Captain is one of the Club's most experienced players, with over ten years' experience of life in the Premier League. He moved from Everton as the transfer window was closing in August 2011.

He can play both as a defensive or attacking midfielder and his passing game is the perfect match for Arsenal's style of play. His intelligence and influence were rewarded when he was made vice-captain at the start of the 2012–13 season.

PLAYER PROFILE

POSITION:	Midfielder
SQUAD NUMBER:	8
DATE OF BIRTH:	26 March 1982
PREVIOUS CLUBS:	Barcelona, PSG (loan), Rangers, Real Sociedad, Everton
ARSENAL DEBUT:	10 September, 2011
INTERNATIONAL TEAM:	Spain (U21)

CHOOSE A COUNTRY

32

IN WHICH COUNTRY HAS ARTETA NOT PLAYED LEAGUE FOOTBALL?
SCOTLAND ☐   **SPAIN** ☐   **SWEDEN** ☐   *Answer on page 94*

Charlie GEORGE

A local London lad, young Charlie had grown up watching Arsenal from the stands. It was a dream come true to make it big at Highbury and the fans took him to their hearts straight away.

Playing up front, Charlie became a regular in the side in the 1970–71 season until a broken ankle slowed his progress. He returned as an attacking midfielder, helping his side to victory in the League Championship that season and scoring five times.

The same season, Arsenal took home the FA Cup with Charlie sealing the win with a spectacular 20-yard shot. It was a dream Double and one of the Gunners' most memorable campaigns.

Position:	Forward/Midfielder
Squad number:	11
Clubs played for:	Derby County, Minnesota Kicks, Southampton, Bulova, Dundee Utd, Coventry City
Arsenal career:	1969–1975
Caps:	179
Goals:	49
International team:	England
International caps:	1

LEGENDS

11

PLAYER PROFILE

MY RATING

COLOUR IN THE STARS TO RATE THIS LEGEND ★ ★ ★ ★ ★

Santi
CAZORLA

19

Creative Cazorla was a key signing for the Gunners in the summer of 2012. The Spanish attacker immediately added flair and style to the Arsenal midfield, as well as goals!

A skilful player, Santi is comfortable playing on either wing or in a central midfield role. Look out for Santi at set pieces – he's scored some sensational goals!

Cazorla has also earned over 50 caps for Spain during the team's most successful spell in their history. Although he missed out on the 2010 World Cup through injury, Super Santi has two European Championship medals to his name.

PLAYER PROFILE

POSITION:	Midfielder
SQUAD NUMBER:	19
DATE OF BIRTH:	13 December 1984
PREVIOUS CLUBS:	Malaga, Recreativo, Villareal, Oviedo
ARSENAL DEBUT:	18 August 2012
INTERNATIONAL TEAM:	Spain

EURO HERO

HOW MANY EUROPEAN CHAMPIONSHIP TITLES HAS CAZORLA WON?
NONE ☐   **ONE** ☐   **TWO** ☐   *Answer on page 94*

Arsenal

David **SEAMAN**

Arsenal's all-time number 1, David Seaman's contribution to George Graham's glory years was massive. Some people questioned his transfer fee of £1.3 million for a keeper but David soon proved he was worth every penny paid for him!

His quick reflexes, positional play and strength helped Arsenal keep 23 clean sheets and concede just 18 goals as the team took the 1990–91 League title. More honours would follow including two more League Championships, four FA Cups, one League Cup and the UEFA Cup Winners' Cup. Wow!

A legend on the International scene too, David won 75 caps for England, playing in two World Cup Finals tournaments.

Position:	Goalkeeper
Squad number:	1
Clubs played for:	Peterborough Utd, Birmingham City, Queens Park Rangers, Manchester City
Arsenal career:	1990–2003
Caps:	564
Goals:	0
International team:	England
International caps:	75

LEGENDS

1

PLAYER PROFILE

MY RATING

COLOUR IN THE STARS
TO RATE THIS LEGEND

★ ★ ★ ★ ★

35

Laurent
KOSCIELNY 6

Another Frenchman, not much was known about Laurent when he joined the Gunners from French club Lorient. He quickly proved himself in Arsenal's defence and justified his eight-figure transfer fee.

Laurent is quick and comfortable with the ball at his feet. He plays in central defence with Per Mertesacker, but can be called upon to play right-back if needed. At 6 foot 1 inch, he's not the tallest defender but has terrific presence in the air.

Since joining Arsenal, Laurent caught the eye of the French national team coach and played for France at Euro 2012.

PLAYER PROFILE

POSITION:	Defender
SQUAD NUMBER:	6
DATE OF BIRTH:	10 September, 1985
PREVIOUS CLUBS:	Guingamp, Tours, Lorient
ARSENAL DEBUT:	15 August, 2010
INTERNATIONAL TEAM:	France

LAURENT'S LOYALTY

36

KOSCIELNY MIGHT HAVE CHOSEN TO PLAY FOR ANOTHER COUNTRY. BUT WHICH ONE...
ANDORRA ☐ BELGIUM ☐ POLAND ☐ *Answer on page 94*

Arsenal

David ROCASTLE

David 'Rocky' Rocastle rose through the junior ranks at Arsenal before becoming a Club legend. With electrifying pace and a venomous shot, this tough central midfielder was a fans' favourite. He won the League Cup before adding two Championship medals to his locker.

In 1992 Rocky was surprisingly transferred to Leeds United in a big-money deal, but injury meant that he never recovered the form of his glory days with the Gunners.

Sadly, David died at the age of just 33, but will never be forgotten at Arsenal. He was a top-class player and a legendary Gunner.

Position:	Midfielder
Squad number:	7
Clubs played for:	Leeds United, Manchester City, Chelsea, Norwich City (loan), Hull City (loan), Sabah
Arsenal career:	1985–92
Caps:	277
Goals:	34
International team:	England
International caps:	14

LEGENDS

7

PLAYER PROFILE

MY RATING

COLOUR IN THE STARS TO RATE THIS LEGEND

★ ★ ★ ★ ★

Aaron
RAMSEY

16

Welsh wonder Aaron was wanted by many Clubs as a youngster. Newcastle, Everton and Manchester United are all reported to have tried to sign him! Aaron opted to move from Cardiff City to Arsenal, though, when he was 17.

Aaron has a clever footballing brain and manager Wenger described the midfielder as 'a player with a fantastic engine, good build, good technique and good vision'.

Ramsey was also given the honour of becoming Wales's youngest-ever captain, when he was 20 years old. In the summer of 2012, he represented Team GB at the Olympic Games in London, too!

PLAYER PROFILE

POSITION:	Midfielder
SQUAD NUMBER:	16
DATE OF BIRTH:	26 December 1990
PREVIOUS CLUBS:	Cardiff City, Nottingham Forest (loan)
ARSENAL DEBUT:	13 August 2008
INTERNATIONAL TEAM:	Wales

ALL-ROUND AARON

38

RAMSEY IS A TOP SPORTSMAN. TAKE A GUESS AT WHICH OTHER SPORT HE COULD HAVE MADE IT AS A PRO.

CRICKET ☐   RUGBY LEAGUE ☐   TENNIS ☐   *Answer on page 94*

Pat RICE

Arsenal

Right-back Rice's Arsenal career really kicked off in his fourth season with the Club when he was a regular in the Double-winning side of 1970–71. He kept his place throughout the 1970s, showing amazing consistency.

Pat later captained Arsenal with real authority, leading them to a hat-trick of FA Cup Finals from 1978 to 1980. Arsenal victoriously brought the Cup home to the Highbury trophy cabinet in 1979.

He moved on after playing over 500 times for the Gunners, but returned to the Club as a coach in 1984. A true Arsenal legend he is remembered for his loyalty and devotion to the Club.

Position:	Defender
Squad number:	2
Clubs played for:	Watford
Arsenal career:	1967–80
Caps:	528
Goals:	13
International team:	Northern Ireland
International caps:	49

LEGENDS

2

PLAYER PROFILE

MY RATING

COLOUR IN THE STARS TO RATE THIS LEGEND

★ ★ ★ ★ ★

39

Bacary SAGNA

3

Before signing Sagna, Arsenal scouts watched the right back play more than 40 times for Auxerre! He impressed in his first season with Arsenal (2007–08) and is known as Mr Reliable by the fans.

When fit, Sagna is one of the first names on the Arsenal team-sheet, thanks to his tough tackling, strong defensive displays and bursts forward with the ball.

He missed out on Euro 2008 and 2012 through injury but did make it to the 2010 World Cup in Japan.

PLAYER PROFILE

POSITION:	Defender
SQUAD NUMBER:	3
DATE OF BIRTH:	14 February 1983
PREVIOUS CLUBS:	Auxerre
ARSENAL DEBUT:	12 August 2007
INTERNATIONAL TEAM:	France

BAC'S A BLUE!

FOR WHICH INTERNATIONAL SIDE DOES BACARY PLAY?
ITALY **SENEGAL** **FRANCE** *Answer on page 94*

Alex JAMES

Scottish forward Alex James has often been compared with Dennis Bergkamp – both these brilliant players had magnificent passing skills and amazing ball control.

Alex liked to play just off the strikers, creating the final balls for legendary team-mates Cliff Bastin and Ted Drake to slot home. He was not known as a goalscorer in his own right, but scored in the 1930 FA Cup Final to help Arsenal claim their first major trophy.

His influence in Arsenal's title-winning campaign the following season was massive too. Three more trophies followed between 1933 and 1935 – a golden period in the Club's history – as Alex kept supplying top scorer Ted Drake.

A career highlight was when Alex captained the Gunners to another FA Cup win in 1936.

Position:	**Midfielder**
Squad number:	**10**
Clubs played for:	**Raith Rovers, Preston North End**
Arsenal career:	**1929–1937**
Caps:	**261**
Goals:	**27**
International team:	**Scotland**
International caps:	**8**

LEGENDS

10

PLAYER PROFILE

MY RATING

COLOUR IN THE STARS TO RATE THIS LEGEND

★ ★ ★ ★ ★

Per MERTESACKER 4

Standing tall at 6 foot 6 inches, Per adds much-needed height to the Gunners' defence. He uses his height well and is worth his weight in gold when set pieces need to be defended.

He signed for Arsenal on transfer deadline day in August 2011 and quickly slotted into the Gunners' backline with some solid displays.

Already an established international when he joined Arsenal, Per has since added more caps for Germany. He hopes to reach the milestone of 100 caps at the 2014 World Cup in Brazil.

PLAYER PROFILE

POSITION:	Defender
SQUAD NUMBER:	4
DATE OF BIRTH:	29 September 1984
PREVIOUS CLUBS:	Hannover 96, Werder Bremen
ARSENAL DEBUT:	10 September 2011
INTERNATIONAL TEAM:	Germany

TRUE OR FALSE?

PER IS TALLER THAN CLUB AND COUNTRY TEAM-MATE, LUKAS PODOLSKI.

TRUE ☐ FALSE ☐ *Answer on page 94*

Bob WILSON

Keeper Bob Wilson was the first amateur player to have a transfer fee paid when he joined Arsenal from Wolves in 1963.

He became the Gunners' first-choice goalie in 1968 thanks to his hard work and intelligent play for the Club. He added the league championship and FA Cup double in the 1970–71 season to the European Fairs Cup medal he had won the previous season with the Gunners.

After he retired through injury at the age of 32, he became Arsenal goalkeeping coach, a job which he did for 28 years, coaching fellow legend David Seaman among others!

Position:	**Goalkeeper**
Squad number:	**1**
Clubs played for:	**Wolverhampton Wanderers**
Arsenal career:	**1963–74**
Caps:	**308**
Goals:	**0**
International team:	**Scotland**
International caps:	**2**

LEGENDS

1

PLAYER PROFILE

MY RATING

COLOUR IN THE STARS
TO RATE THIS LEGEND

★ ★ ★ ★ ★

NACHO
MONREAL
17

Ignacio Monreal Eraso, or 'Nacho' as he is nicknamed, is one of Arsenal's latest recruits, having joined the Club on the final day of the winter transfer window in 2013.

Known for his high work rate, the left back is full of stamina and able to get up and down the wing super-fast. His style of play perfectly matches Arsenal's, as Nacho loves to take short, sharp touches and has excellent movement off the ball.

He helped his previous Club, Malaga, qualify for the Champions League for the first time in their history, alongside team-mate Santi Cazorla.

PLAYER PROFILE

POSITION:	Defender
SQUAD NUMBER:	17
DATE OF BIRTH:	26 February 1986
PREVIOUS CLUBS:	Osasuna, Malaga
ARSENAL DEBUT:	2 February 2013
INTERNATIONAL TEAM:	Spain

DREAM DEFENDER

IN WHICH DEFENSIVE POSITION DOES NACHO PLAY?
LEFT BACK ▢ RIGHT BACK ▢ GOALKEEPER ▢ Answer on page 94

Arsenal *Freddie* LJUNGBERG

A free-scoring midfielder, stylish Freddie made himself an Arsenal favourite with the fans when he scored just seconds into his debut against Manchester United! His runs from deep on either wing were his trademark style of play, but Freddie's best role was just behind the strikers.

Fans also loved the bright red stripe in Freddie's hair, which he dyed to match his Gunners' kit!

A key member of the Invincibles, Freddie won two Premier League titles with Arsenal, three FA Cups and three Community Shields. That's one mighty medal collection!

He won 75 caps for his country, playing for Sweden for a whole decade.

Position:	**Midfielder**
Squad number:	**8**
Clubs played for:	**Halmstads BK, West Ham Utd, Seattle Sounders, Chicago Fire, Celtic, Shimzu S-Pulse**
Arsenal career:	**1998–2007**
Caps:	**328**
Goals:	**72**
International team:	**Sweden**
International caps:	**75**

LEGENDS

8

PLAYER PROFILE

MY RATING

COLOUR IN THE STARS TO RATE THIS LEGEND ★★★★★

Alex OXLADE-CHAMBERLAIN

15

Following in the footsteps of team-mate Theo Walcott, Alex burst onto the scene at Arsenal as a 17-year-old from Southampton. He's a strong, exciting attacking player who can play centrally or in wide areas.

Alex made his debut as a substitute in the away game against Manchester United, and scored quality goals in his next two appearances for Arsenal.

He's also a member of the England senior squad, like his father, Mark Chamberlain, before him. Look out for the Ox at Arsenal for years to come!

PLAYER PROFILE

POSITION:	Midfielder/Forward
SQUAD NUMBER:	15
DATE OF BIRTH:	15 August 1993
PREVIOUS CLUBS:	Southampton
ARSENAL DEBUT:	28 August 2011
INTERNATIONAL TEAM:	England

NAME GAME

ALEX HAS THE LONGEST NAME OF ALL THE ARSENAL SQUAD, BUT WHAT IS WRITTEN ON THE BACK OF HIS PLAYING SHIRT?

OXLADE-CHAMBERLAIN ☐   ALEX ☐   CHAMBERLAIN ☐   *Answer on page 94*

Robert PIRÈS

INVINCIBLE

Robert 'Bobby' Pirès made a huge contribution in the six seasons he spent at Highbury. Upon joining Arsenal, Pirès had already been victorious at the World Cup in 1998 and Euro 2000 playing for his country, France. He was the perfect replacement for Marc Overmars, who had left the Club the previous summer.

A gutsy, passionate midfielder, Pirès had an excellent touch. He linked up on the left in a tremendous trio with Ashley Cole and Thierry Henry to produce some sublime goals. Bobby netted an enviable 84 goals in total and won seven major honours with the Gunners. A sensational number 7!

Position:	Midfielder
Squad number:	7
Clubs played for:	Metz, Marseille, Villareal, Aston Villa
Arsenal career:	2000–2006
Caps:	284
Goals:	84
International team:	France
International caps:	79

LEGENDS

7

PLAYER PROFILE

MY RATING

COLOUR IN THE STARS TO RATE THIS LEGEND ★ ★ ★ ★ ★

47

GERVINHO 27

Ivorian striker Gervinho attracted attention after winning the league with French side, Lille.

He's a tricky striker to play against and has pace on his side. Gervinho loves to take on defenders and dribbling is another of his main weapons.

Although his name sounds Brazilian, 'Gervinho', or Gervais Yao Kouassi comes from Africa and he plays his international football for the Ivory Coast.

Whether playing for Club or country, the African ace is both a goalscorer and provider for his team-mates.

PLAYER PROFILE

POSITION:	Forward
SQUAD NUMBER:	27
DATE OF BIRTH:	27 May 1987
PREVIOUS CLUBS:	Beveren, Le Mans, Lille
ARSENAL DEBUT:	13 August 2011
INTERNATIONAL TEAM:	Ivory Coast

COAST TO COAST

GERVINHO HAS MADE OVER 45 APPEARANCES FOR...
BRAZIL ☐ IVORY COAST ☐ PORTUGAL ☐ *Answer on page 94*

Ray PARLOUR

INVINCIBLE

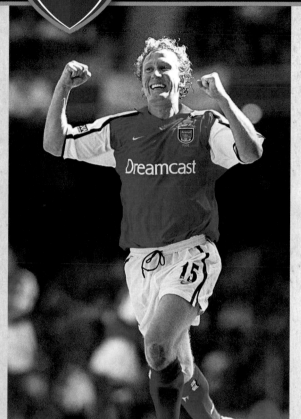

A Gunner through and through, Ray's best footballing years were with Arsenal. He was a hard-working and tough-tackling midfielder.

Manager George Graham gave the young Parlour his big break, after Ray had first joined the Club as a trainee.

The arrival of Wenger at the Club helped Ray really develop his game. He was a star player on the right or in central midfield when Arsenal won the double in the 1997–98 season, and was Man of the Match in the FA Cup Final that year.

By the end of his time with the Gunners, Parlour had won three League titles, four FA Cups, one League Cup and one European Cup Winners' Cup. He may not have got the plaudits of some of his team-mates, but 466 appearances for Arsenal definitely puts Parlour in the Legends category.

Position:	Midfielder
Squad number:	15
Clubs played for:	Middlesbrough, Hull City
Arsenal career:	1992–2004
Caps:	466
Goals:	32
International team:	England
International caps:	10

LEGENDS

15

PLAYER PROFILE

MY RATING

COLOUR IN THE STARS
TO RATE THIS LEGEND

★ ★ ★ ★ ★

Arsène Wenger

Wenger masterminds a 6–2 win over Blackburn in 2009.

Did you know?
Wenger was the Gunners' first manager from outside the UK.

When Frenchman Wenger arrived in north London in 1996, little was known about Arsenal's new manager. Few predicted the French Revolution that would follow, changing Arsenal's history forever.

In his first season with the Club, he steered Arsenal to third place in the Premier League. 1997–98 was Wenger's first full season in charge. He introduced new training regimes and healthy diets for his squad and soon reaped the rewards as Arsenal won the Double.

His style of play – creative, attacking football – brought more trophies as Arsenal did it again, winning the Double in 2001–02 and another FA Cup in 2003.

The following season was the best yet as Arsenal made history by completing the whole Premier League season without losing a single game. Wenger's team that went on to play 49 matches unbeaten became known as the 'Invincibles'.

Arsène on the ball!

50

Arsène has brought some legendary players into the Club including Thierry Henry, Nicolas Anelka, Marc Overmars, Cesc Fabregas, Robert Pirès and Theo Walcott. He also has a talent for getting the best out of young players – Cesc Fabregas, Mathieu Flamini and Kolo Touré all made their names while at Arsenal.

European glory was almost in Arsène's grasp when he led his team to the 2006 Champions League Final. The Gunners may have lost to Barcelona on the night, but Wenger's desire to become the champions of Europe remains as strong as ever.

(Above) Arsène is adored by the fans!

(Below) Wenger lifts the Premier League trophy in the Double-winning season 2001–02

Taking in the atmosphere at the new Emirates Stadium.

Did you know?
Arsène is the longest-serving manager in the Premier League!

MANAGER PROFILE

ARSENAL CAREER:	1 October 1996–present
ARSENAL DEBUT AS MANAGER:	12 October 1996, Blackburn Rovers 0–2 Arsenal
DATE OF BIRTH:	22 October 1949
PREVIOUS CLUBS MANAGED:	Nancy–Lorraine, AS Monaco, Nagoya Grampus Eight
NATIONALITY:	French
NICKNAME:	Le Professeur (The Teacher)

ARSENAL TROPHIES (SO FAR!)

FA Premier League: 1997–98, 2001–02, 2003–04   **FA Cup:** 1998, 2002, 2003, 2005
FA Community Shield: 1998, 1999, 2002, 2004

MY DREAM TEAM

You've swotted up on the current stars and read about the legends. Now it's time to create your own squad of Arsenal superstars!

Who will make it into your dream team? You can choose any player you like, from any time in the Club's history. Will you include an awesome Invincible or even pick yourself in the starting XI?

LB Marcelo

GK M. Neuer

CB Gibbs

CB Ramos

RB Monreal

Subs' Bench

MANAGER Dylan Heath

SUBS

LM Bale

CM Ozil

CM Walcott

RM Ronaldo

CF Sanchez

CF Henry

53

PUZZLES: Half time!

Spot the Difference

Here's Olivier Giroud celebrating a goal in the Champions League!

Can you find 6 differences between the pictures?

Sudoku Squares

Check your answers to all the puzzles on pages 94 and 95!

Try this picture Sudoku to test your smart skills! Remember, each picture can appear only once in each column, row and box.

PUZZLES: Half time!

Memory Test

Think you have a good memory? Time to put it to the test! Study everything on this page for two minutes then cover this page and look at page 57.

GUNNER
99

SUPER TOUGH!

Now grab a piece of paper and see how much you can remember by answering the ten questions below.

1 How many footballs were on the page?

2 Which way was the cannon facing?

3 What colour kit was Szczesny wearing?

4 How many trophies did you count?

5 What colour were Thomas Vermaelen's boots?

6 How many players were wearing the Arsenal home kit?

7 Who was wearing a training kit?

8 How many corner flags were there?

9 What shirt number was Gunnersaurus wearing?

10 Which player was number 15?

Gunners A-Z

How well do you know your Club?

Check out this guide from A to Z for a lowdown on life at Arsenal FC.

A is for... Arsenal

One of the most famous teams in the world, Arsenal Football Club has existed for over 125 years. Nicknamed 'the Gunners', Arsenal aim to make their fans proud by playing stylish football with passion in every game.

B is for... Bergkamp

Arguably the classiest player ever to pull on an Arsenal shirt, Dennis Bergkamp's brilliance was clear for all to see. Dennis the Menace ran rings around defenders, leaving opposition fans open-mouthed!

Bergkamp on the ball in his testimonial match at Emirates Stadium.

C is for... Chapman

If you ask an older fan who the best manager Arsenal has ever had was, they may well say Herbert Chapman. The Club had never won a trophy when he joined in 1925, but Chapman won the FA Cup and two league titles with Arsenal before his sudden death in 1934. His Gunners team went on to win five more league titles in the 1930s.

Chapman's bust.

D is for... Dressing Room

The home dressing room at the Emirates is shaped like a horseshoe so that all the players can hear the manager's team talks – Arsène Wenger helped to design it! Its other state-of-the-art facilities include a warm-up area, spa baths and cushioned seats for the players. Luxury!

E is for... Emirates Stadium

Arsenal moved to the awesome Emirates back in 2006 from the legendary Highbury, which is just down the road!

F is for... Fabregas

Arsenal's youngest-ever player, and youngest-ever scorer, Cesc Fabregas's 212 appearances and 35 goals for the Gunners means he will never be forgotten by the fans. Wenger gave Fabregas the captain's armband when Cesc was just 21 years old.

G is for... Gunnersaurus

Gunner, or Gunnersaurus Rex to call him by his full name, is Arsenal's dino matchday mascot. A friend to all Junior Gunners, it's Gunnersaurus's job to warm up the crowd before kick-off. He's also got a seriously good left foot!

H is for... Henry

Thierry Henry joined Arsenal from Italian club Juventus back in 1999 for a hefty £11 million fee. He started out as a left-winger, but clever Wenger moved him up to play as a striker, where Henry went on to smash Arsenal's all-time goal-scoring record. A legend.

I is for... Invincibles

The 2003–04 season saw Wenger's boys achieve something truly remarkable – they became the first Premier League team to remain unbeaten for a whole season! The group of players was so feared that they became known as the 'Invincibles'.

J is for... Junior Gunners

The Junior Gunners are Arsenal's youngest fans and are some of the loudest supporters the Club has! Junior Gunners often get to be matchday mascots and attend exclusive events with the players. Check out www.arsenal.com/juniorgunners if you'd like to sign up!

K is for... Keown

Another rock in Arsenal's defence, Martin Keown notched up over 400 appearances for the Gunners between 1993 and 2004. He won the double twice, under managers Graham and Wenger, and was known for his thunderous tackling.

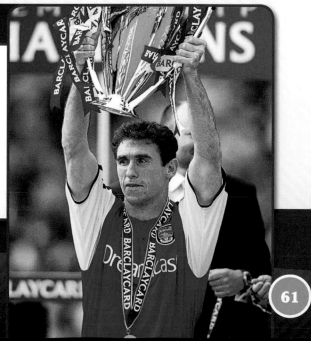

61

L is for... Ladies

The famous Arsenal Ladies FC were founded in 1987, and can proudly claim to be the best Club in English women's football!
This talented team has won over 30 major trophies, including a domestic and European quadruple in 2007! They play their games at Meadow Park in Borehamwood, a ground that can pack in over 4,500 fans.

M is for... McLintock

Scottish stopper Frank McLintock earned cult hero status while playing for Arsenal thanks to him leading the Club to its first double in the 1970–71 season.
He also captained the Gunners in the Inter-Cities Fairs Cup final, where Arsenal beat Anderlecht 3–1.

N is for... North Bank

The North Bank at Highbury was home to some of the Gunners' most passionate supporters during Arsenal's 93-year stay at the ground. The famous stand had a capacity of 12,500 – the biggest of Highbury's four terraces. It was bombed during World War II and had to be rebuilt. During this time Arsenal had to play their home games at White Hart Lane!

O is for... O'Leary

Irish defender David O'Leary holds the record for having played the most number of games of any Arsenal player. He was one of the first names on the team sheet for almost 20 years! He made 722 appearances for the Gunners, playing as a centre back.

P is for... Premier League

Since the Premier League kicked off in 1992, Arsenal have earned a hat-trick of league titles, including two league and cup doubles! Did you know that the Gunners have only had three managers since the Premier League was set up – George Graham, Bruce Rioch and of course mega manager, Arsène Wenger!

The best-ever Premier League team collecting their prize in 2004!

Q is for... Quality

With some of the most technically gifted players in the league, Arsenal stand out for the way they play their football. Arsène Wenger's squad is packed with stylish players, who play the Arsenal way – a passing game with quality and passion.

Thierry Henry, perhaps Arsenal's most stylish-ever striker?

R is for... Result!

No matter the score line, you can rest assured that Arsenal go for the win in every single game in which they play. From nail-biting 1–0 narrow victories to romping walkovers, the aim is always the same – to take all three points.

The Emirates' scoreboard displaying Arsenal's record result in the Champions League.

S is for... Seaman

An excellent signing, David Seaman kept goal for Arsenal during the George Graham years and beyond, winning honour after honour. His final act as an Arsenal player, after earning 564 appearances and eight major trophies, was to lift the FA Cup in 2003 as captain of the Gunners following a 1–0 win over Southampton.

T is for... Tottenham Hotspur

Archrivals, Tottenham Hotspur are based only 6 km away from Emirates in north London! The rivalry between the Gunners and Spurs dates back over 100 years, resulting in some passionate derby matches when the two sides come head to head each season.

U is for... Unbeaten run

Arsenal's 49 game unbeaten run in the Premier League remains the English record. With a brilliant string of results, the Gunners well and truly rewrote the record books between 7 May 2003 and 16 October 2004. They only failed to score in 4 of the 49 games, with Henry scoring 36 by himself!

V is for... Vieira

Frenchman Patrick Vieira was an early signing for new manager Arsène Wenger back in 1996 and took no time to settle into English football – he swept the Gunners to double glory in his first full season. A powerful midfielder and influential player, Wenger made Vieira captain in summer 2002.

W is for... Wenger

'The Professor' has been the boss of Arsenal since September 1996. Not much about him was known when he arrived in English football, but today Arsène Wenger is one of the game's most respected managers, having won 11 trophies with the Gunners. He is one of the cleverest gaffers around in the transfer market, with an ability to spot the potential in young players, helping to transform them into world-class legends.

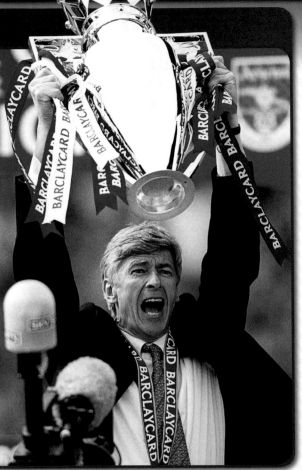

X is for... XI

Who would make it into your first XI of all-time great Arsenal players? See what it's like to be a manager and pick out your own fantasy dream team on pages 52–53. You can choose players from any period in Arsenal's history for your squad – past legends or today's heroes!

Y is for... Youth

The philosophy at Arsenal is all about youth. If a player is good enough, age will not stop them getting into the first team. The Gunners' youngest-ever first-team player was Cesc Fabregas at just 16 years, 256 days, closely followed by Jack Wilshere, who made his league debut at 16 years, 329 days.

Z is for... Zero

Zero is the amount of years that Arsenal have been out of the top flight since the 1920s. No other team has spent more consecutive seasons in the top flight, which is a record. Zero is also the number of goals the Gunners hope to concede each matchday!

0

Team Profile: Arsenal Ladies

WINNERS

The FA WSL
Continen
CUP FIN

Arsenal Ladies FC were formed in 1987 and have been nothing short of sensational ever since! With 38 trophies in 25 years, Arsenal has a Ladies team of which it can be proud.

The team likes to play attractive, attacking football and, like all the best teams, has a good balance of youth and experience.

Arsenal Ladies' most successful season was 2006–07 when they won a historic Quadruple in their 20th anniversary year! This season they will be gunning for the big one once again – the UEFA Women's Champions League.

12 Women's Premier League Titles

2 Women's Super League

1 UEFA Women's Champions League

10 Women's Premier League Cups

11 FA Women's Cups

5 Women's Community Shields

2 WSL Continental Cup

10 London County FA Women's Cup

STAR PLAYERS

Kelly SMITH

Kelly is one of the squad's most experienced players and has seen the women's game grow in the UK over the years. She has also spent time abroad playing in the USA. Kelly is a natural-born striker and plays as a striker for the Gunners. England's record goalscorer with 45 goals, Kelly has also earned over 100 caps for her country, after first making her debut at 17.

PLAYER PROFILE

POSITION:	Forward
SQUAD NUMBER:	10
DATE OF BIRTH:	October 29, 1978
PREVIOUS CLUBS:	Wembley, Seton Hall Pirates, Philadelphia Charge, New Jersey Wildcats, Boston Breakers
ARSENAL HONOURS:	UEFA Cup, Super League, four Premier League titles, three FA Cups, five League Cups
INTERNATIONAL TEAM:	England

Steph HOUGHTON

Young defender Steph won the Treble with Arsenal in her very first season at the Club! A calm and talented stopper, Steph can also play in midfield when needed and has even played as a striker during her career! Steph starred for Team GB in the London 2012 Olympic Games when she was named left back of the tournament.

PLAYER PROFILE

POSITION:	Defender/Midfielder
SQUAD NUMBER:	2
DATE OF BIRTH:	April 23, 1988
PREVIOUS CLUBS:	Sunderland, Leeds Carnegie
ARSENAL HONOURS:	two Super League titles, two Super League Cups, FA Women's Cup
INTERNATIONAL TEAM:	England

SOCCER SCHOOLS
PLAY THE ARSENAL WAY™

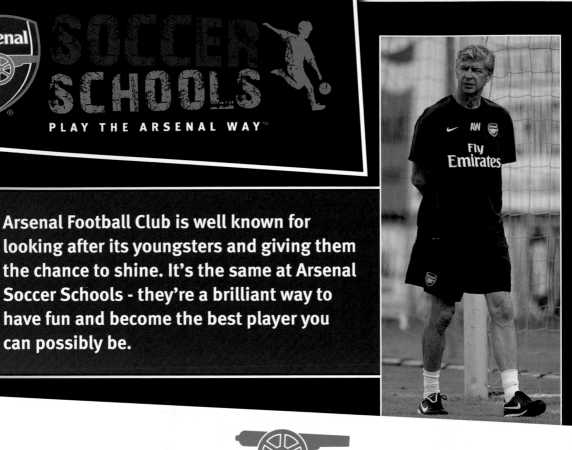

Arsenal Football Club is well known for looking after its youngsters and giving them the chance to shine. It's the same at Arsenal Soccer Schools - they're a brilliant way to have fun and become the best player you can possibly be.

Here at Arsenal Football Club we pride ourselves on playing as a team to produce imaginative, entertaining and skilful football. We take time to develop and nurture our younger players to ensure that they reach their full potential. By guiding players through our extensive training programmes, we have produced many world-class players over the years, something that we are very proud of.

Arsenal Soccer Schools have been operating since 1985 around the UK and have expanded internationally. The courses are based on the same principles used at the training ground, developing young players' technical skills and passion for the game to ensure they become the best players they possibly can.

Our soccer school courses welcome children of all abilities and it doesn't matter which team the children support, we just want everyone to have fun while learning to play football the Arsenal way!

Arsène Wenger

Visit www.playthearsenalway.com to find your nearest soccer school!

A – ATTITUDE

To progress to your full potential as a football player it is vital to have the correct attitude both on and off the football pitch. You need to be as positive and dedicated as possible to fully master your skills and you need to be cool and composed when under pressure to keep control of the moment you're in.

R – RESPECT

Always respect your teammates, your opponent, your coach and the referee. In order to get the best out of your team it's important to appreciate the efforts of those around you. If you fail to respect the opponent you underestimate their potential, which can make your own standards fall below your usual level. Football should be played in the spirit of fair play, encouragement and fun. Take advice from your coach to help your game improve and remember self-respect is key for your own development as a player and a person.

S – SKILLS

At Arsenal we believe that skills and technique are essential to inspire creativity, flair, excitement and entertainment. Skills can help make football fun, help you improve as a player and help you beat your opponent. Be inventive with the turns and tricks you use to move the ball, use both feet and don't forget to work on the basic skills such as control and passing.

E – ENERGY

You need to have lots of energy to get the most out of playing football. The longer you can maintain a high level of fitness, the more this will benefit you in games. If you're not as fit as you can be, it becomes difficult to play to your maximum level. Drink plenty of water, avoid junk food and be as active as you can in your day-to-day lives.

N – NEW THINKING

Embrace your coach's ideas and always think about different ways you can improve tactically and technically. Be creative with your thoughts and express them on the field whenever you can.

A – ALL FOR ONE

As much as you can work on your own development, football is a team game. The more you work with your teammates the better you will become as a player and a team. It doesn't matter who you are or where you're from, football is a game that can be played by everyone. Enjoy the feeling of belonging to a team and do all you can to help your team-mates.

L – LEARNING

Learn how to play the Arsenal way: football based around passing and movement, technique and skill. Incorporating the principles of fair play, teamwork, expression and fun!

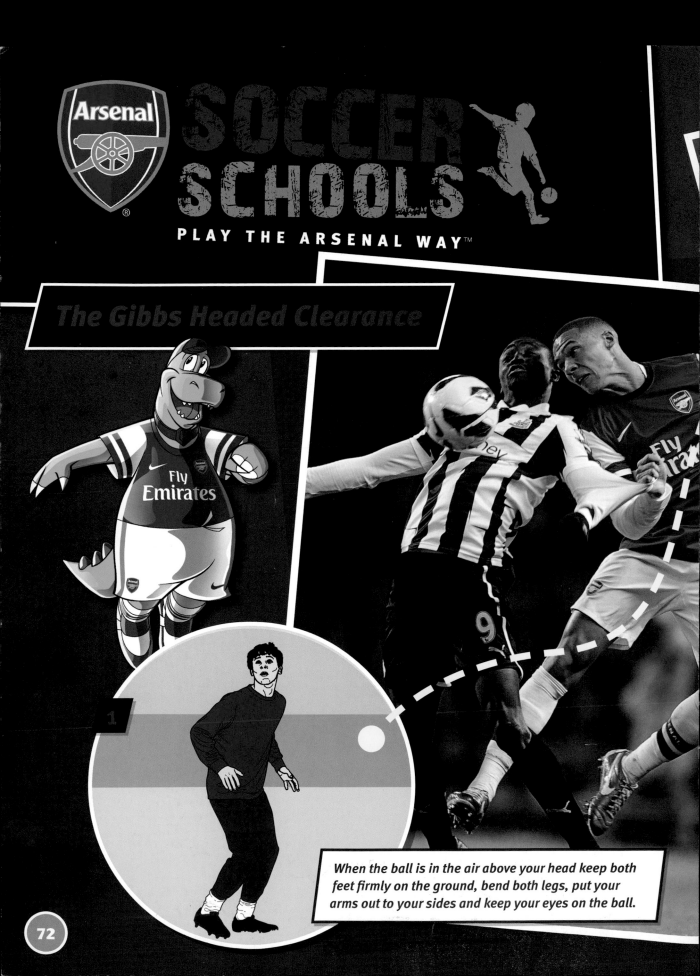

Arsenal SOCCER SCHOOLS

PLAY THE ARSENAL WAY™

The Gibbs Headed Clearance

1

When the ball is in the air above your head keep both feet firmly on the ground, bend both legs, put your arms out to your sides and keep your eyes on the ball.

2

Extend your arms further out to protect yourself and to support your jump. Open your body slightly and bend your back leg to help your spring.

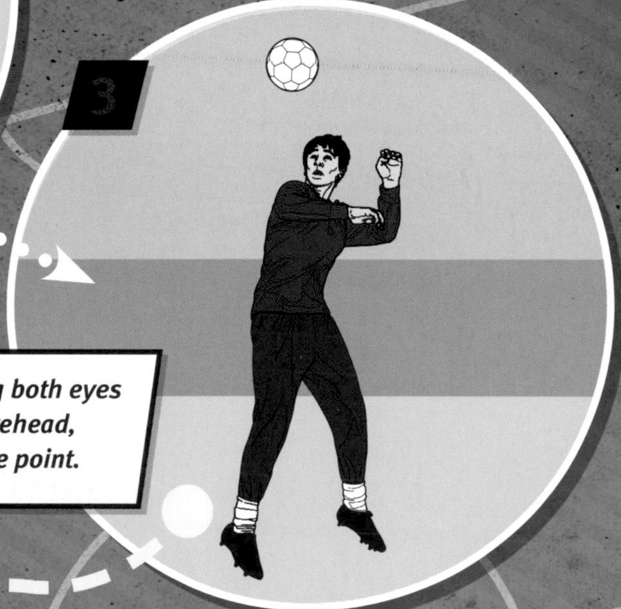

3

Leap off the ground and keeping both eyes on the ball connect with your forehead, meeting it at the highest possible point.

4

Connect with the lower underside of the ball and use your neck muscles to attack the ball and to help you get as much height and distance as possible.

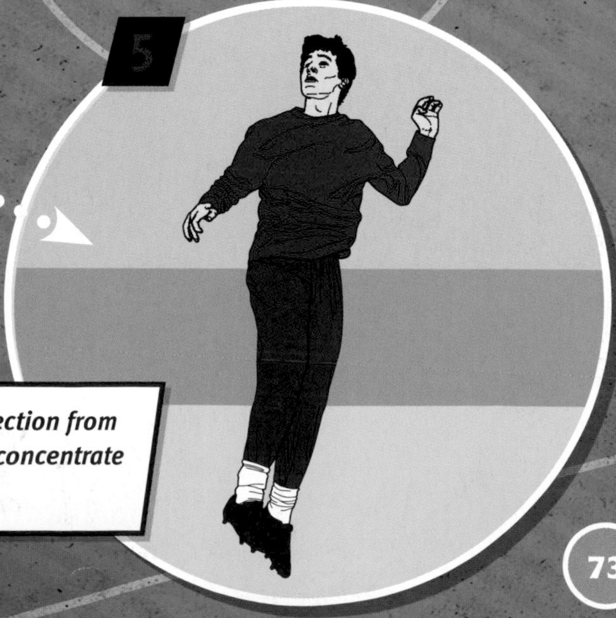

5

Keep your arms out for balance and protection from other players competing for the ball and concentrate on making a steady landing on both feet.

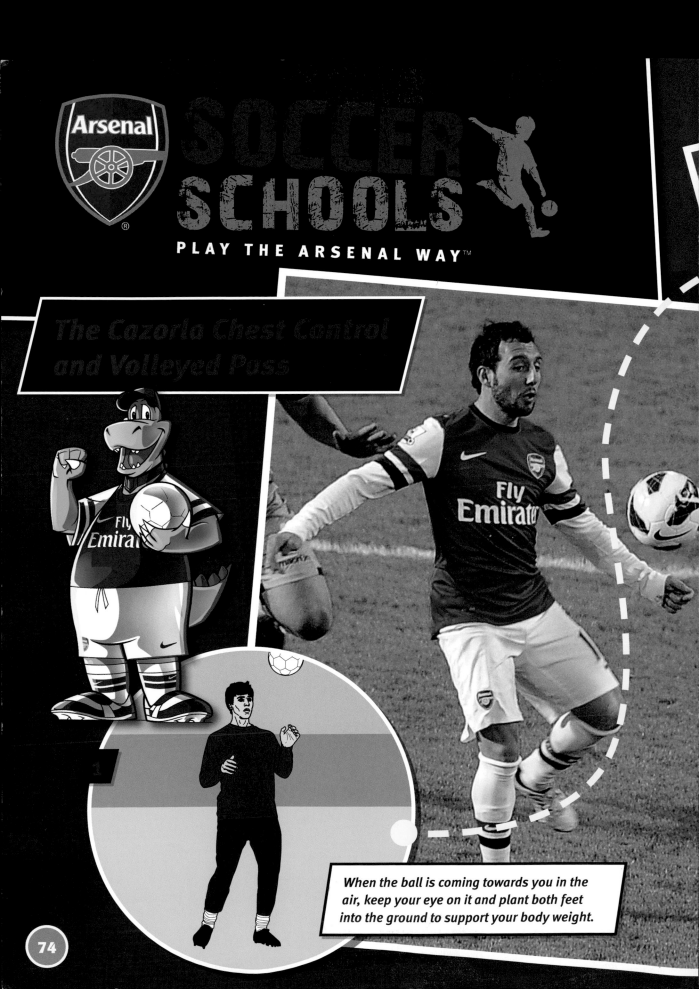

SOCCER SCHOOLS
PLAY THE ARSENAL WAY™

The Cazorla Chest Control and Volleyed Pass

When the ball is coming towards you in the air, keep your eye on it and plant both feet into the ground to support your body weight.

2

Raise your arms to the front to help your balance, and make sure your chest area is as wide as it can be.

3

Arch your back so that your chest faces upwards and cushion the ball with your chest so that the pace is taken off and the ball moves slightly upwards after contact.

4

As the ball is rising, take a step backwards and plant your non-kicking foot into the ground, raising your kicking foot towards the ball as it starts to move towards the ground. Take a quick look at where you want the ball to go.

5

Keep your eyes on the ball and swing your kicking foot through in the direction of where the ball is dropping.

6

Turn your foot so that the inside makes contact with the ball while it is still in the air. Follow through with your foot moving in the same direction as where you passed the ball.

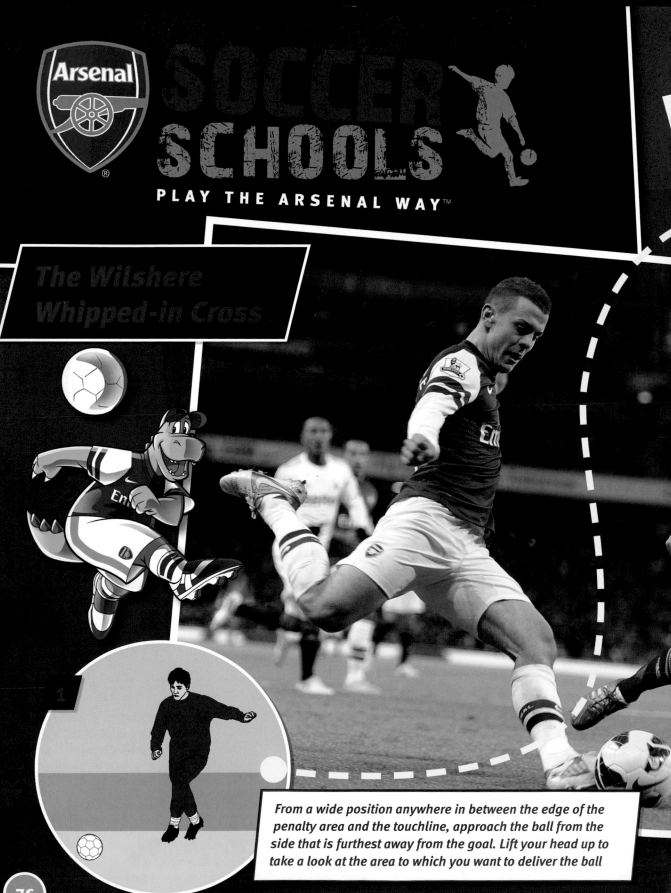

SOCCER SCHOOLS

PLAY THE ARSENAL WAY™

The Wilshere Whipped-in Cross

1

From a wide position anywhere in between the edge of the penalty area and the touchline, approach the ball from the side that is furthest away from the goal. Lift your head up to take a look at the area to which you want to deliver the ball

2

Plant your non-kicking foot just behind the ball and bend your kicking leg so that your heel on that foot bends behind you – this generates the power to move the ball as you connect with it.

3

Put both arms out to your side to help keep your balance. Bring your kicking foot down towards the ball so that as your leg straightens to make contact, your foot moves in a crescent/arc shape towards the ball.

4

Lean back slightly to help lift the ball off the ground.

5

Using your instep make contact with the ball just below the centre in order to elevate the flight of the ball and twist your hips in the direction that you want the ball to move in. The arc of your foot's movement should ensure that the ball spins through the air, bending as it travels.

6

After making contact with the ball follow through with the kicking movement, plant both feet and be ready to move again with the play.

SOCCER SCHOOLS

PLAY THE ARSENAL WAY™

The Walcott Rollover

Move your body into a position as if you're going to play a pass to a team-mate, lifting your arm for balance.

78

2 Plant your non-kicking foot to the side of the ball and bend this leg to take most of your weight and generate power into the pass.

3 Lift your kicking foot and move it towards the ball.

4 Using your instep make contact with the top of the ball – not the centre as you would if you were passing. Roll your foot over the top from one side of the ball to the other so that your foot never loses contact with the ball, but the point of contact changes from your instep to your sole, to the outside of your foot.

5 Using the outside of your foot push the ball away from you in the opposite direction to the way your foot was moving.

6 Bend your legs to help generate power.

7 Accelerate away, keeping the ball under enough control so that it doesn't move too far away from you.

8 Move off into space in the direction you have turned.

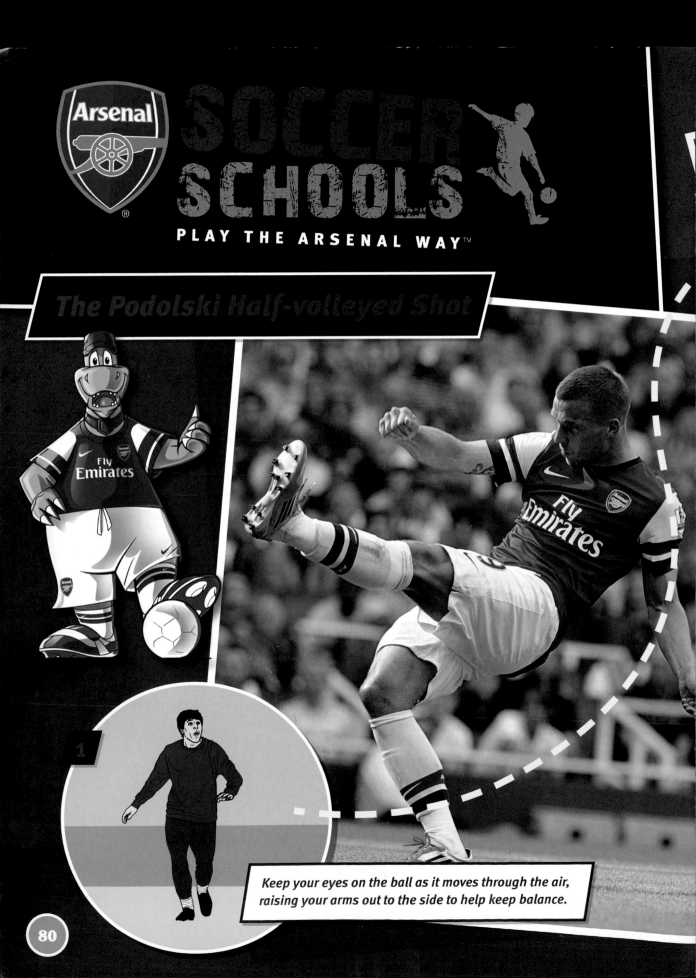

SOCCER SCHOOLS
PLAY THE ARSENAL WAY™

The Podolski Half-volleyed Shot

1

Keep your eyes on the ball as it moves through the air, raising your arms out to the side to help keep balance.

2 Pull back your striking foot so that your heel moves towards your backside.

3 Swing your foot forward so that you are in a position to make contact with the ball.

4 As the ball is about to hit the ground keep your ankle locked and toes pointing down. Connect with the ball the instant it touches the ground.

5 Follow through, keeping your foot moving in the direction of the ball.

MY SKILLS
RECORD

TICK OFF THE SKILLS BELOW ONCE YOU HAVE STUDIED THEM AND PRACTISED THEM YOURSELF. THEN ADD A TOUGHNESS RATING FOR EACH SKILL!

The Gibbs Headed Clearance

Toughness: ⭐ 1 ⭐ 2 ⭐ 3 ⭐ 4 ⭐ 5

The Cazorla Chest Control and Volleyed Pass

Toughness: ⭐ 1 ⭐ 2 ⭐ 3 ⭐ 4 ⭐ 5

The Wilshere Whipped-in Cross

Toughness: ⭐ 1 ⭐ 2 ⭐ 3 ⭐ 4 ⭐ 5

The Walcott Rollover

Toughness: ⭐ 1 ⭐ 2 ⭐ 3 ⭐ 4 ⭐ 5

The Podolski Half-Volleyed Shot

Toughness: ⭐ 1 ⭐ 2 ⭐ 3 ⭐ 4 ⭐ 5

TROPHY CABINET

From the Club's first silverware in the 1930s to the glory of the George Graham years and Arsène's amazing Invincibles... Read on for a complete guide to how all of Arsenal's trophies were won – it's quite a journey!

1930
Arsenal beat Huddersfield Town 2–0 in the FA Cup at Wembley. Legendary manager Herbert Chapman is in charge, and Alex James and Jack Lambert score the Gunners' goals.

1931
Arsenal become the first southern team to win the League, and rack up a new Club record of 127 goals!

1933
More silverware, as Arsenal win their second ever League title.

1934
Arsenal are crowned back-to-back League Champions. Sadly, Chapman dies, with George Allison replacing him as manager.

1935
Allison makes it three in a row as the Gunners retain their status as Champions.

1936
Sharp-shooter Ted Drake scores as Arsenal beat Sheffield United 1–0 to win the FA Cup at Wembley.

1938
Another title for the Gunners as they finish a point ahead of Wolves to clinch the League.

1948
After a decade without silverware, new manager Tom Whittaker leads Arsenal to their sixth League title. The superstars of the day were Ronnie Rooke, Joe Mercer and George Swindin.

1950
Playing in gold jerseys at Wembley, the Gunners beat a Liverpool side 2–0.

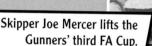

Skipper Joe Mercer lifts the Gunners' third FA Cup.

1953
Arsenal secure a seventh League title by the narrowest of victories – the league was decided by goal average over the season.

1970
After a 17-year wait for silverware, Arsenal win the Inter-Cities Fairs Cup Final, beating Anderlecht to win their first European trophy.

1971
A golden Gunners season as they triumph in both the League and FA Cup. Star players include Frank McLintock and Charlie George.

McLintock on the shoulders of Charlie George and Pat Rice.

1979

A fifth FA Cup is won in a Wembley thriller! Over 99,000 fans watch Alan Sunderland score a last-minute winner to give Arsenal a 3–2 victory over Manchester United.

1987

A new era begins as Arsenal win their first silverware under George Graham, beating Liverpool in the League Cup Final 2–1. Charlie Nicholas scores both goals.

1989

Heroics on the last day of the season at Anfield secure the League for Graham's Gunners. Michael Thomas got his name in the history books by scoring a stoppage-time winner! Phew!

1991

An amazing tenth League title! Not much got past the Gunners' mean defence and striker Alan Smith netted 22 goals.

1993

Arsenal become the first Club to win both domestic Cups. They beat Sheffield Wednesday both times!

1994

The Gunners win their sixth trophy under George Graham, this time in Europe. Arsenal beat Italian side Parma 1–0 in Copenhagen.

1998

Arsène Wenger's first full season at Arsenal is a spectacular one as the Club wins the Premier League and FA Cup Double!

2002

The Gunners win another incredible Double under Wenger! They're crowned champions at Old Trafford, and beat Chelsea 2–0 at the Millennium Stadium to win the FA Cup.

2003

A single Robert Pirès goal lands the FA Cup again for Arsenal, as they beat Southampton 1–0!

2004

Arsenal's most memorable season of the modern age, as the team of 'Invincibles' wins the League unbeaten, with a Club record 90 points.

The Invincibles in action.

2005

The FA Cup final against Man United finishes goalless after extra time. The Gunners become the first Club to win the Cup in a nail-biting penalty shoot-out, 5–4. Epic!

PUZZLES: Full time!

Who Am I?

Can you tell which member of the current squad is talking? As soon as you know, write the name in the space, followed by the letter of the clue you got.

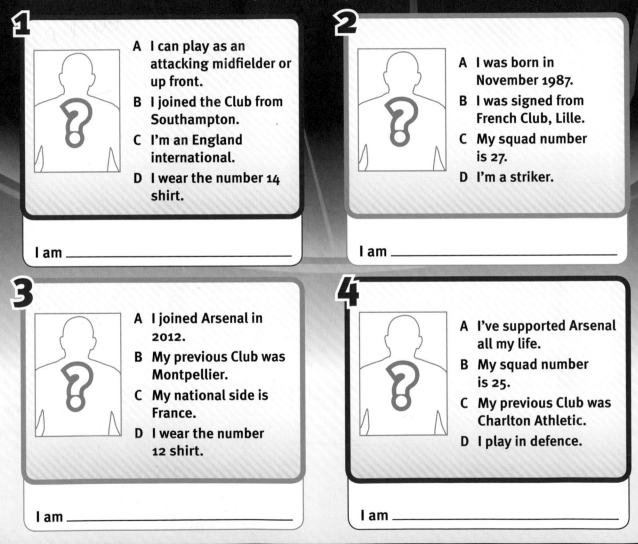

1

A I can play as an attacking midfielder or up front.

B I joined the Club from Southampton.

C I'm an England international.

D I wear the number 14 shirt.

I am _____

2

A I was born in November 1987.

B I was signed from French Club, Lille.

C My squad number is 27.

D I'm a striker.

I am _____

3

A I joined Arsenal in 2012.

B My previous Club was Montpellier.

C My national side is France.

D I wear the number 12 shirt.

I am _____

4

A I've supported Arsenal all my life.

B My squad number is 25.

C My previous Club was Charlton Athletic.

D I play in defence.

I am _____

HOW DID YOU SCORE?

Mostly As – Expert alert! Not many could rival you as a true Arsenal fan.

Mostly Bs – Outstanding performance! You really know your stuff.

Mostly Cs – Good effort: you're a proud fan.

Mostly Ds – Read through the book again to improve your Gunners knowledge!

Odd One Out

Check your answers to all the puzzles on pages 94 and 95!

Take a look at these 6 all-action shots. Can you spot which one is different from the rest?

A

B

C

D

E

F

PUZZLES: Full time!

Number Crunchers

Do you know your squad numbers? Work out which missing player completes the sum, then write the number on the shirt and the player's name above it.

GIROUD
12

KOSCIELNY
6

PODOLSKI
9

B WILSHERE 10 − ? = ARTETA 8

C ? − SZCZESNY 1 = RAMSEY 16

D ? − MERTESACKER 4 = CHAMBERLAIN 15

E ? + ARTETA 8 + SZCZESNY 1 = ARSHAVIN 23

Face in the Crowd

Gunner has decided to join the fans on matchday! Can you spot where he's hiding in the Emirates' crowd?

Motto Mix-up

On a piece of paper try to unscramble the official Arsenal motto.
Tip: if you need some help the motto is written somewhere in the book!

TICYORV GOHTHUR ROYMAHN

Highbury
Stadium Tour

The pitch was always kept in top condition by a team of groundsmen.

Home to the Gunners for almost a century, the historic Highbury Stadium was where titles were won, goals were scored and heroes were made.

The first competitive match at Highbury was played on 6 September 1913. Woolwich Arsenal beat Leicester Fosse 2–1.

The ground was redeveloped in the 1930s when a spectacular grandstand for 17,000 fans was built. No expense was spared as the famous marble hall with a bronze bust of former manager, Herbert Chapman, was opened. It was one of the most luxurious grounds in the country!

At its peak Highbury's capacity was 73,000, though when it closed there was only room to seat about half that number of fans. A bigger stadium was needed for the future of the Club and its fans, and construction on a new home began in February 2004.

Players and fans were sad to see Highbury close its doors for a final time on Sunday 7 May 2006. A magnificent ceremony, including a parade of Arsenal legends and a fireworks display, was a fitting way to close the stadium.

The home changing room at Highbury, where so many legendary players prepared for matches.

ARSENAL

Highbury and Emirates Stadium stand just half a mile apart!

The famous Arsenal clock was moved from Highbury to Emirates Stadium and sits high above the south end of the stadium, now known as the 'Clock End'. It was lifted into place by a 25-tonne crane and took four people nine hours to install!

Arsenal is the only Club in London to have a tube station named after them. When Highbury was grandly renovated in the 1930s the station changed its named from Gillespie Road to Arsenal, and is still used today by fans travelling on matchdays.

Did you know?
The North Bank Terrace was bombed during World War II and had to be completely rebuilt.

MEMORABLE MATCHES

From record scores to last-minute winners, we look back at some of the most magnificent Arsenal performances of the last decade. Do you remember any of these matches? Ask the older Gunners in your family if they do, too!

2002–03 Season

DATE:
4 MAY 2002

SCORE:
ARSENAL 2
CHELSEA 0

COMPETITION:
FA CUP FINAL

A special day in the Club's history, the Gunners' FA Cup victory over London rivals Chelsea gave the team a taste for victory – just five days later they would win the Premier League and a complete a double Double for manager, Wenger. Played at the Millennium Stadium, late goals from Ray Parlour and Freddie Ljungberg sealed the win and Arsenal's eighth FA Cup.

2003–04 Season

INVINCIBLE SEASON

DATE:
15 MAY 2004

SCORE:
ARSENAL 2
LEICESTER CITY 1

COMPETITION:
PREMIER LEAGUE

With so many memorable matches in a campaign when Arsenal went unbeaten, the Gunners ended their season with a narrow win over Leicester City. The last match of the Invincibles campaign may not be a classic, but this didn't matter – everyone at Highbury was in the mood to party! It was fitting that captain Patrick Vieira scored the winner before collecting the Premier League trophy at the end of the match. Highbury history!

DATE:
21 MAY 2005

SCORE:
ARSENAL 0
MANCHESTER UTD 0
(5–4 ON PENALTIES)

COMPETITION:
FA CUP FINAL

A tough encounter at the Millennium Stadium, which was still 0–0 after extra time. Thierry Henry was out injured, and lone striker Dennis Bergkamp failed to break the deadlock. When it went to the dreaded penalty shoot-out Arsenal kept their cool, scoring all five of their penalty kicks. Vieira's decisive spot-kick meant that Arsenal would become the first side to win the FA Cup on penalties.

The players celebrate winning a nail-biting match!

2003 — 2004

DATE:
17 MAY 2006

SCORE:
BARCELONA 2
ARSENAL 1

COMPETITION:
CHAMPIONS LEAGUE
FINAL

Although it was Highbury's farewell season, it is a match played in Paris that stands out. In a remarkable run that had seen Arsenal go 10 matches and 995 minutes without conceding a goal in the Champions League, Arsenal lined up against European giants Barcelona in the Final. Arsenal keeper Jens Lehmann was unluckily sent off in the first half, but Arsenal took the lead with a thumping Sol Campbell header. Barcelona broke Gunners' hearts in the second half, though, scoring twice in the last 14 minutes to deny Arsenal their first European Cup.

How Arsenal lined up on the night.

DATE:
23 OCTOBER 2007

SCORE:
ARSENAL 7
SLAVIA PRAGUE 0

COMPETITION:
CHAMPIONS LEAGUE

A night when everything Arsenal touched turned to gold! An 18-year-old Theo Walcott, playing only his second match up front for Arsenal, struck twice after Fabregas had opened the scoring. Then an own goal plus another from Alex Hleb had the fans dancing in their seats! When Bendtner scored a seventh he equalled Arsenal's best-ever victory in European Competition, and this final goal rounded off an incredible performance.

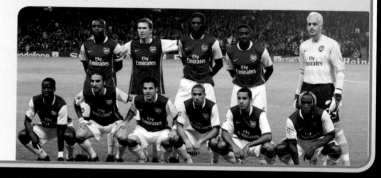

DATE:
21 APRIL 2009

SCORE:
LIVERPOOL 4
ARSENAL 4

COMPETITION:
PREMIER LEAGUE

Despite the memorable home win over Manchester United and a well-fought victory at Chelsea that season, Liverpool away will live long in the memories of Gunners fans. The game had everything – cards, free-flowing football and EIGHT goals to count! Andrey Arshavin delivered a vintage performance with all four goals before Liverpool equalised in stoppage time. Stunning!

DATE:
15 AUGUST 2009

SCORE:
EVERTON 1
ARSENAL 6

COMPETITION:
PREMIER LEAGUE

On the opening day of a new season Arsenal truly hammered Everton at Goodison Park! At one point in the match they were leading 5–0 as the Gunners went goal crazy with strikes from Denilson, Vermaelen, Gallas and Fabregas (2). Everton pulled one back before Eduardo scored a sixth. Arsène Wenger quite rightly called his players 'superheroes' in his post-match interview!

Gallas grabs the Gunners' third.

DATE:
1 MAY 2011

SCORE:
ARSENAL 1
MANCHESTER UTD 0

COMPETITION:
PREMIER LEAGUE

In a season that didn't quite live up to the high standards set by Wenger's men, this home win late in the campaign put a smile back on the fans' faces. Aaron Ramsey's second-half strike helped the Gunners secure a Champions League spot.

A single strike from Aaron Ramsey ensures the Arsenal win.

DATE:
29 OCTOBER 2011

SCORE:
CHELSEA 3
ARSENAL 5

COMPETITION:
PREMIER LEAGUE

A thriller to delight Arsenal's loyal away fans at Stamford Bridge! Three goals from former striker Robin van Persie, plus Santos and Walcott goals saw Chelsea slump to an unexpected defeat. Alan Hansen described the match as 'one of the best matches you will ever see'!

An outstanding away performance!

DATE:
29 DECEMBER 2012

SCORE:
ARSENAL 7
NEWCASTLE UTD 3

COMPETITION:
PREMIER LEAGUE

On 29 December 2012, 60,000 fans crammed into Emirates Stadium to watch a Christmas cracker of a game! Walcott scored a hat-trick and Giroud bagged a brace coming on as a substitute for the last 15 minutes! Podolski and the Ox scored the other two. Was it Thierry Henry watching from the stands that inspired the Gunners' goals? Either way, it was another awesome Arsenal performance and a vital three points won.

Olivier Giroud scoring Arsenal's fifth!

PUZZLES: Answers

Page 12
SPOT THE BALL
The ball is in A6

DID YOU KNOW?
p20. false, p22. 2012, p24. 8, p26. speed, p28. Koscielny, p30. his brother, p32. Sweden, p34. two, p36. Poland, p38. Rugby League, p40. France, p42. true, p44. left back, p46. Chamberlain, p48. Ivory Coast.

Page 54
SPOT THE DIFFERENCE
Walcott's badge and foot have disappeared; Ramsey's boots have changed colour and the number is missing from his shorts; Giroud's finger is missing; words have disappeared from the hoarding.

Page 13
SOCCER SCRAMBLE
1. Ian Wright, 2. David Seaman, 3. Liam Brady, 4. Thierry Henry, 5. Robert Pirès, 5. Tony Adams.

Page 14
CORNER CLOSE-UPS

Page 15
HELP GUNNER!
The players are Jack Wilshere and Aaron Ramsey